The NFL's Greatest Teams

LOS ANGELES RAMS

Big Buddy Books

An Imprint of Abdo Publishing
abdopublishing.com

Katie Lajiness

abdopublishing.com

Published by Abdo Publishing, a division of ABDO, PO Box 398166, Minneapolis, Minnesota 55439. Copyright © 2017 by Abdo Consulting Group, Inc. International copyrights reserved in all countries. No part of this book may be reproduced in any form without written permission from the publisher. Big Buddy Books™ is a trademark and logo of Abdo Publishing.

Printed in the United States of America, North Mankato, Minnesota.
092016
012017

Cover Photo: ASSOCIATED PRESS.
Interior Photos: ASSOCIATED PRESS (pp. 5, 7, 9, 11, 13, 14, 15, 17, 18, 19, 20, 21, 24, 25, 27, 29);
  Ron Niebrugge/Alamy Stock Photo (p. 23).

Coordinating Series Editor: Tamara L. Britton
Graphic Design: Michelle Labatt, Taylor Higgins, Jenny Christensen

Publisher's Cataloging-in-Publication Data

Names: Lajiness, Katie, author.
Title: Los Angeles Rams / by Katie Lajiness.
Description: Minneapolis, MN : Abdo Publishing, 2017. | Series: NFL's greatest
    teams | Includes bibliographical references and index.
Identifiers: LCCN 2016944882 | ISBN 9781680785371 (lib. bdg.) |
    ISBN 9781680798975 (ebook)
Subjects: LCSH: Los Angeles Rams (Football team)--History--Juvenile
    literature.
Classification: DDC 796.332--dc23
LC record available at http://lccn.loc.gov/2016944882

Contents

A Winning Team

The Los Angeles Rams are a football team from Los Angeles, California. They have played in the National Football League (NFL) for more than 80 years.

The Rams have had good seasons and bad. But time and again, they've proven themselves. Let's see what makes the Rams one of the NFL's greatest teams.

Blue, gold, and white are the team's colors.

5

League Play

Team Standings

The NFC and the American Football Conference (AFC) make up the NFL. Each conference has a north, south, east, and west division.

The NFL got its start in 1920. Its teams have changed over the years. Today, there are 32 teams. They make up two conferences and eight divisions.

The Rams play in the West Division of the National Football Conference (NFC). This division also includes the Arizona Cardinals, the San Francisco 49ers, and the Seattle Seahawks.

The San Francisco 49ers are major rivals of the Rams.

Fans get excited to watch the Rams play!

Kicking Off

The Rams joined the NFL in 1937. The team was based in Cleveland, Ohio. They did not have a winning record for their first six seasons. In 1943, the Rams stopped play because of **World War II**.

The Rams returned to the NFL in 1944. Again, they didn't win many games. The Rams finally found success in 1945. They won their first NFL **championship**!

The Rams played the Washington Redskins in the 1945 championship game. At the time, this was the coldest NFL championship game ever played. The temperature was −8°F (−22°C).

In 1948, the Rams were the first professional team to feature a symbol or logo on their helmets.

Highlight Reel

The Rams moved to Los Angeles in 1946. They won the NFL **championship** again in 1951. The team's popularity grew. Many fans went to see the Rams play home games.

The team made it to the play-offs every year from 1973 to 1979. And, they appeared in five NFC championship games. In 1980, the Rams played in their first Super Bowl!

Their success continued during the 1980s. The Rams made it to the play-offs seven times. But, they never made it back to the Super Bowl.

Win or Go Home

NFL teams play 16 regular season games each year. The teams with the best records are part of the play-off games. Play-off winners move on to the conference championships. Then, conference winners face off in the Super Bowl!

The 1980 Super Bowl was played at the Rose Bowl in Pasadena, California. The Pittsburgh Steelers beat the Rams 31–19.

In 1995, the team moved to Saint Louis, Missouri. They struggled the first four years there. Then in 2000, the Rams played in their second Super Bowl. They beat the Tennessee Titans 23–16!

The Rams had another great year in 2002. They made it the Super Bowl for the third time! Sadly, they lost to the New England Patriots 20–17.

In 2016, the Rams announced they would move back to Los Angeles. They are the only team in NFL history to win **championships** in three cities!

Many fans are excited for the Rams to return to Los Angeles.

Quarterback Kurt Warner was the Most Valuable Player (MVP) of the 2000 Super Bowl.

Halftime! Stat Break

Team Records

RUSHING YARDS
Career: Steven Jackson, 10,138 yards (2004–2012)
Single Season: Eric Dickerson, 2,105 yards (1984)
PASSING YARDS
Career: Jim Everett, 23,758 yards (1986–1993)
Single Season: Kurt Warner, 4,830 yards (2001)
RECEPTIONS
Career: Isaac Bruce, 942 receptions (1994–2007)
Single Season: Isaac Bruce, 119 receptions (1995)
ALL-TIME LEADING SCORER
Jeff Wilkins, 1,223 points (1997–2007)

Famous Coaches

George Allen (1966–1970)
Mike Martz (2000–2005)

Championships

EARLY CHAMPIONSHIP WINS:
1945, 1951
SUPER BOWL APPEARANCES:
1980, 2000, 2002
SUPER BOWL WINS:
2000

Fan Fun

STADIUM: Los Angeles Memorial Coliseum
LOCATION: Los Angeles, California
MASCOT: Rampage

Pro Football Hall of Famers & Their Years with the Rams

George Allen, Coach (1966–1970)
Eric Dickerson, Running Back (1983–1987)
Marshall Faulk, Running Back (1999–2005)
Tom Fears, End (1948–1956)
Kevin Greene, Linebacker/Defensive End (1985–1992)
Elroy Hirsch, Halfback/End (1949–1957)
David "Deacon" Jones, Defensive End (1961–1971)
Tom Mack, Guard (1966–1978)
Ollie Matson, Halfback (1959–1962)
Merlin Olsen, Defensive Tackle (1962–1976)
Orlando Pace, Tackle (1997–2008)
Dan Reeves, Owner (1941–1971)
Les Richter, Linebacker (1954–1962)
Jackie Slater, Tackle (1976–1995)
Norm Van Brocklin, Quarterback (1949–1957)
Bob Waterfield, Quarterback (1945–1952)
Jack Youngblood, Defensive End (1971–1984)

Coaches' Corner

George Allen's coaching style turned losing teams into winners. In 1966, he joined the Rams. During his first year, the Rams earned an 8–6 record. During his **career**, he led the team to five successful seasons. In 2002, Allen became a member of the Pro Football Hall of Fame.

In 2000, Mike Martz became head coach. Under his leadership, the Rams made four play-offs. And, they won two division titles and played in the 2002 Super Bowl!

Allen was President Richard Nixon's favorite football coach.

In 2002, Martz led the Rams to an NFC championship.

Jeff Fisher took over as head coach in 2012.

Star Players

Bob Waterfield QUARTERBACK (1945–1952)

In 1945, Bob Waterfield led the Rams to a 9–1 record. In the NFL **championship** game, Waterfield threw two touchdown passes to beat the Washington Redskins. In 1965, Waterfield became the first Rams player to join the Pro Football Hall of Fame.

Tom Fears END (1948–1956)

Tom Fears scored the winning touchdown in the 1951 NFL title game. Throughout his **career** with the Rams, Fears completed 400 receptions for 5,397 yards. And, he made 38 touchdowns. In 1970, Fears joined the Pro Football Hall of Fame.

Merlin Olsen DEFENSIVE TACKLE (1962–1976)

The Rams picked Merlin Olsen in the first round of the 1962 **draft**. Olsen was the leader of the team's defensive line known as the Fearsome Foursome. He was chosen to play in the Pro Bowl, which is the NFL's all-star game, 14 years in a row. This is tied for an NFL record!

Jack Youngblood DEFENSIVE END (1971–1984)

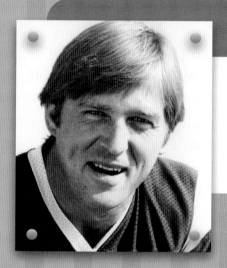

Jack Youngblood was with the Rams his whole **career**. He played 201 straight games with the team. Youngblood even played when he was injured! He was invited to play in the Pro Bowl seven straight years.

Eric Dickerson RUNNING BACK (1983–1987)

In 1983, Eric Dickerson was chosen in the first round of the **draft**. During his first year, he set three different rushing records for a **rookie**. At the end of the season, Dickerson was named Offensive Rookie of the Year. The next year, he rushed for 2,105 yards and set an NFL record and a team record.

Marshall Faulk RUNNING BACK (1999–2005)

Marshall Faulk joined the Rams in 1999. That year, he scored 12 touchdowns and rushed for 1,381 yards. Faulk helped the Rams become Super Bowl **champions** in 2000. During his seven years with the team, Faulk was named NFL Offensive Player of Year three times and MVP once!

Todd Gurley RUNNING BACK (2015–)

Todd Gurley's **rookie** season was great! He set an NFL record by running for 566 yards in his first four games. By the end of the season, he had rushed 229 times for 1,106 yards and ten touchdowns. Gurley was named Offensive Rookie of the Year.

Los Angeles Memorial Coliseum

The Rams play home games at the Los Angeles Memorial Coliseum. It opened in 1923. The stadium can hold up to 92,000 people.

22

The Los Angeles Memorial Coliseum hosted two Olympic Games and two Super Bowls.

Go Rams!

Thousands of fans flock to the Los Angeles Memorial Coliseum to see the Rams play home games. The team's **mascot** is Rampage. He helps cheer on the Rams at home games.

Some Rams fans wear carved-out watermelons on their heads. These fans are called Melonheads!

Rampage makes more than 300 appearances a year. He has even traveled to Alaska and Hawaii!

Final Call

The Rams have a long, rich history. They won NFL **championships** in three cities.

Even during losing seasons, true fans have stuck by them. Many believe the Los Angeles Rams will remain one of the greatest teams in the NFL.

In 2016, Case Keenum became the starting quarterback for the Rams.

Through the Years

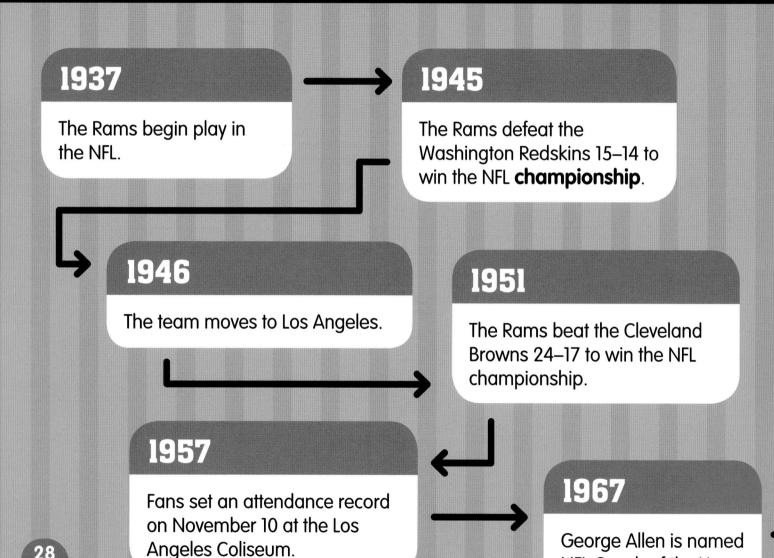

1937
The Rams begin play in the NFL.

1945
The Rams defeat the Washington Redskins 15–14 to win the NFL **championship**.

1946
The team moves to Los Angeles.

1951
The Rams beat the Cleveland Browns 24–17 to win the NFL championship.

1957
Fans set an attendance record on November 10 at the Los Angeles Coliseum.

1967
George Allen is named NFL Coach of the Year.

28

1980

The Rams play the Pittsburgh Steelers in the Super Bowl. The Rams lose 31–19.

1995

The Rams move to Saint Louis.

2000

The team beats the Tennessee Titans to win the Super Bowl 23–16!

2002

The Rams lose in the Super Bowl to the New England Patriots, 20–17.

2016

The Rams move back to Los Angeles.

Postgame Recap

1. What is the name of the stadium where the Rams play home games?
   A. O.co Coliseum   **B**. Los Angeles Memorial Coliseum
   C. Coleman Coliseum

2. Name 2 of the 17 Rams in the Pro Football Hall of Fame.

3. What year did the Rams win the Super Bowl?
   A. 1999
   B. 2000
   C. 2001

4. Who coached the Rams during the 2002 Super Bowl?
   A. Mike Martz
   B. George Allen
   C. Jeff Fisher

1. B. 2. See page 15. 3. B. 4. A.

Glossary

career a period of time spent in a certain job.

champion the winner of a championship, which is a game, a match, or a race held to find a first-place winner.

draft a system for professional sports teams to choose new players.

mascot something to bring good luck and help cheer on a team.

rookie a first-year player in a professional sport.

World War II a war fought in Europe, Asia, and Africa from 1939 to 1945.

Websites

To learn more about the NFL's Greatest Teams, visit **booklinks.abdopublishing.com**. These links are routinely monitored and updated to provide the most current information available.

Index